DOT-to-DOT Books for kids

Ages 4-8

This Book belongs to :

....

....

7
6
5
4
3
2
1

1
2
3
4
5
6
7

1
2
3
4
5
6
7

7
6
5
4
3
2
1

1
2
3
4
5
6
7

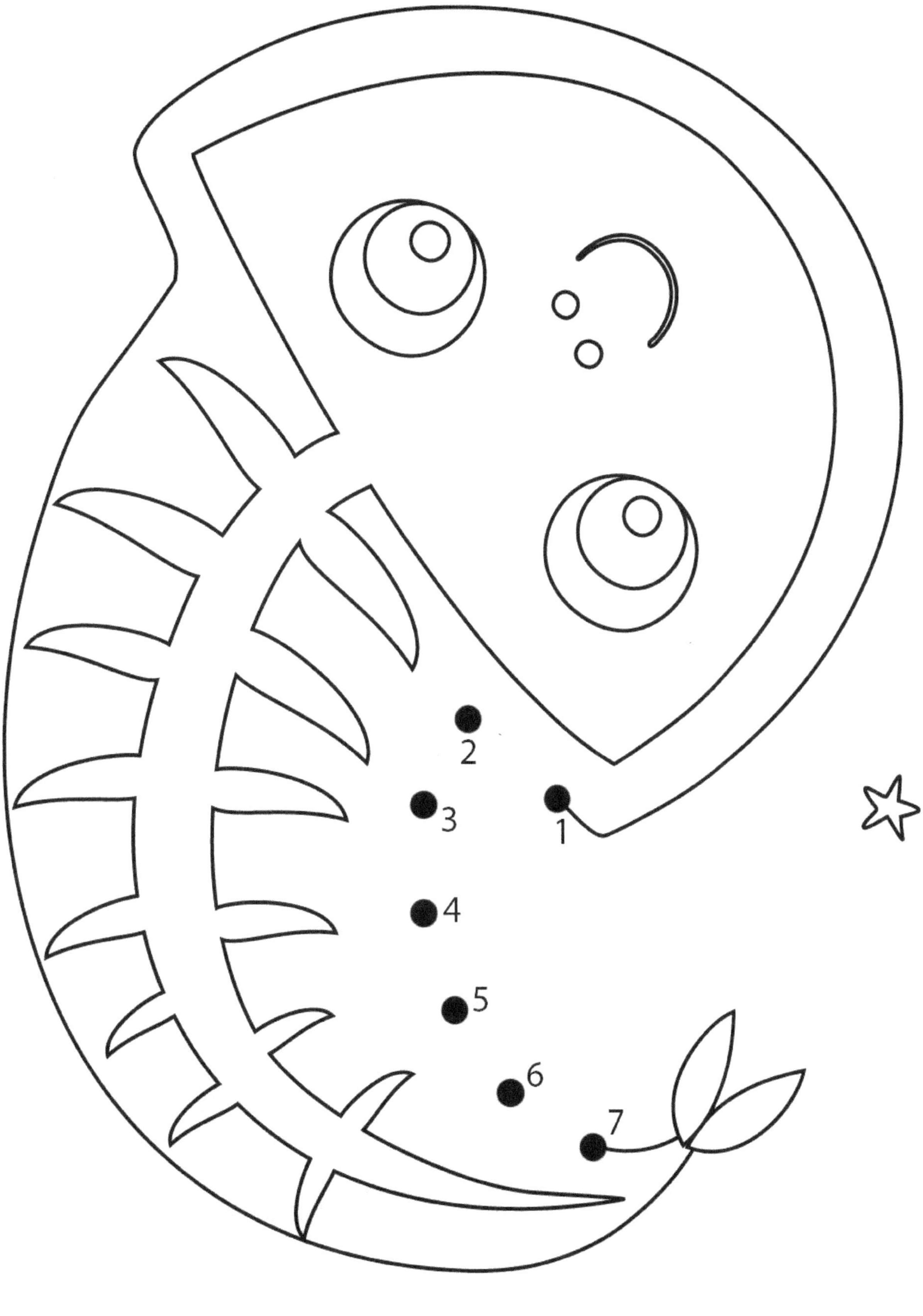
1
2
3
4
5
6
7

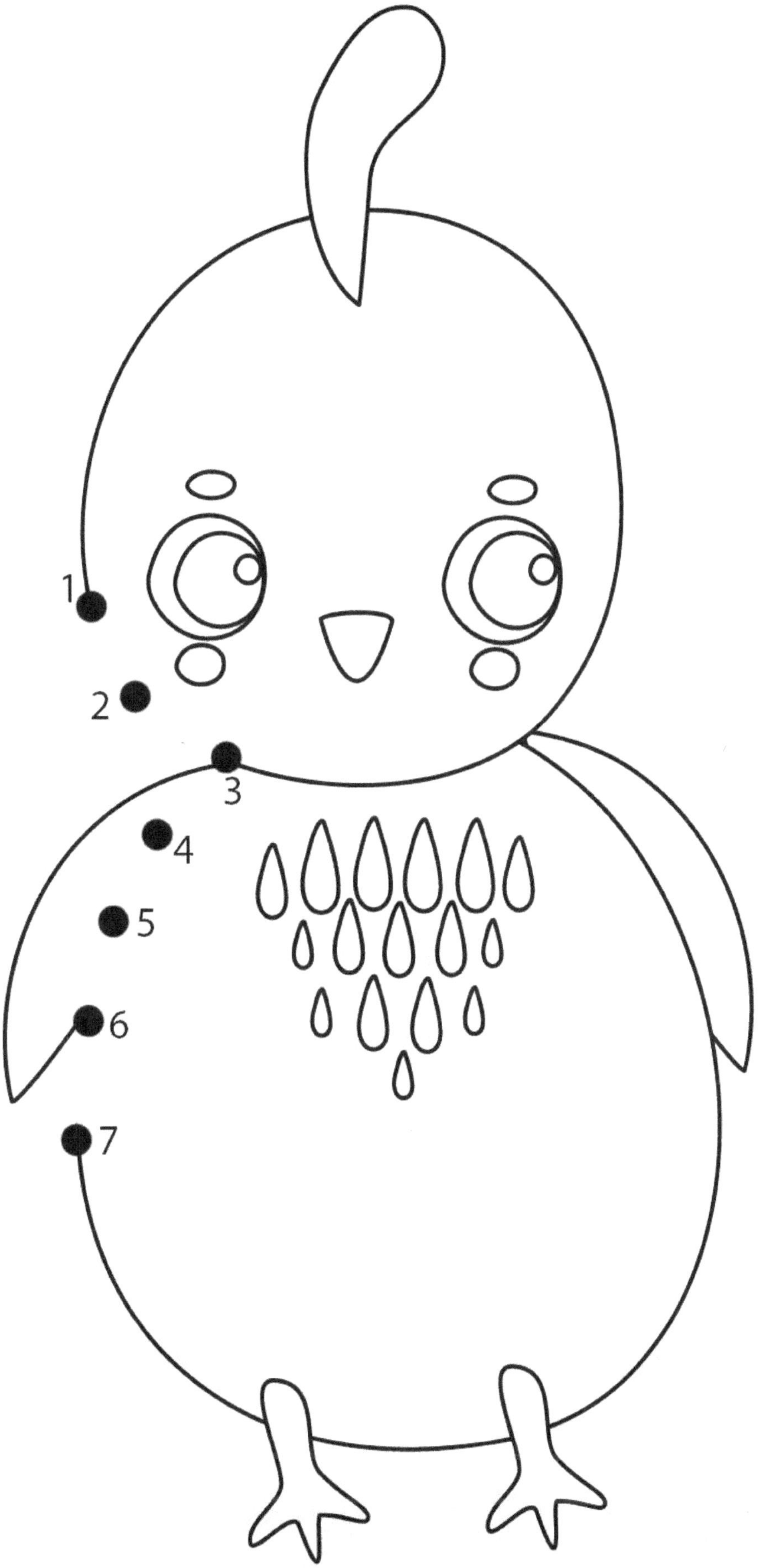
1
2
3
4
5
6
7

1
2
3
4
5
6
7

1
2
3
4
5
6
7

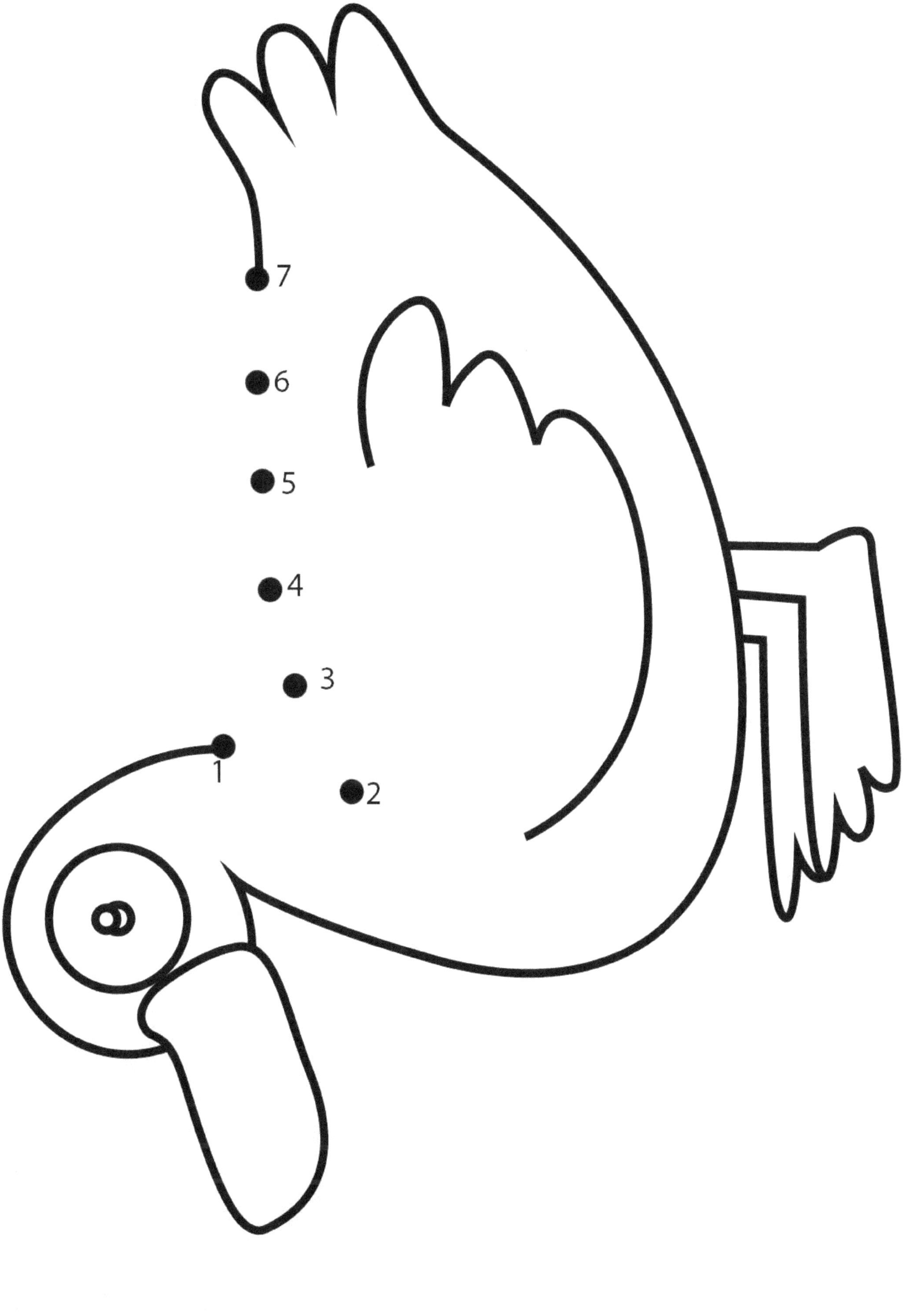
7
6
5
4
3
1
2

1
6
2
7
3
5
4

1
2
3
4
5
6
7

1
2
3
4
5
6
7

1
2
3
4
5
6
7

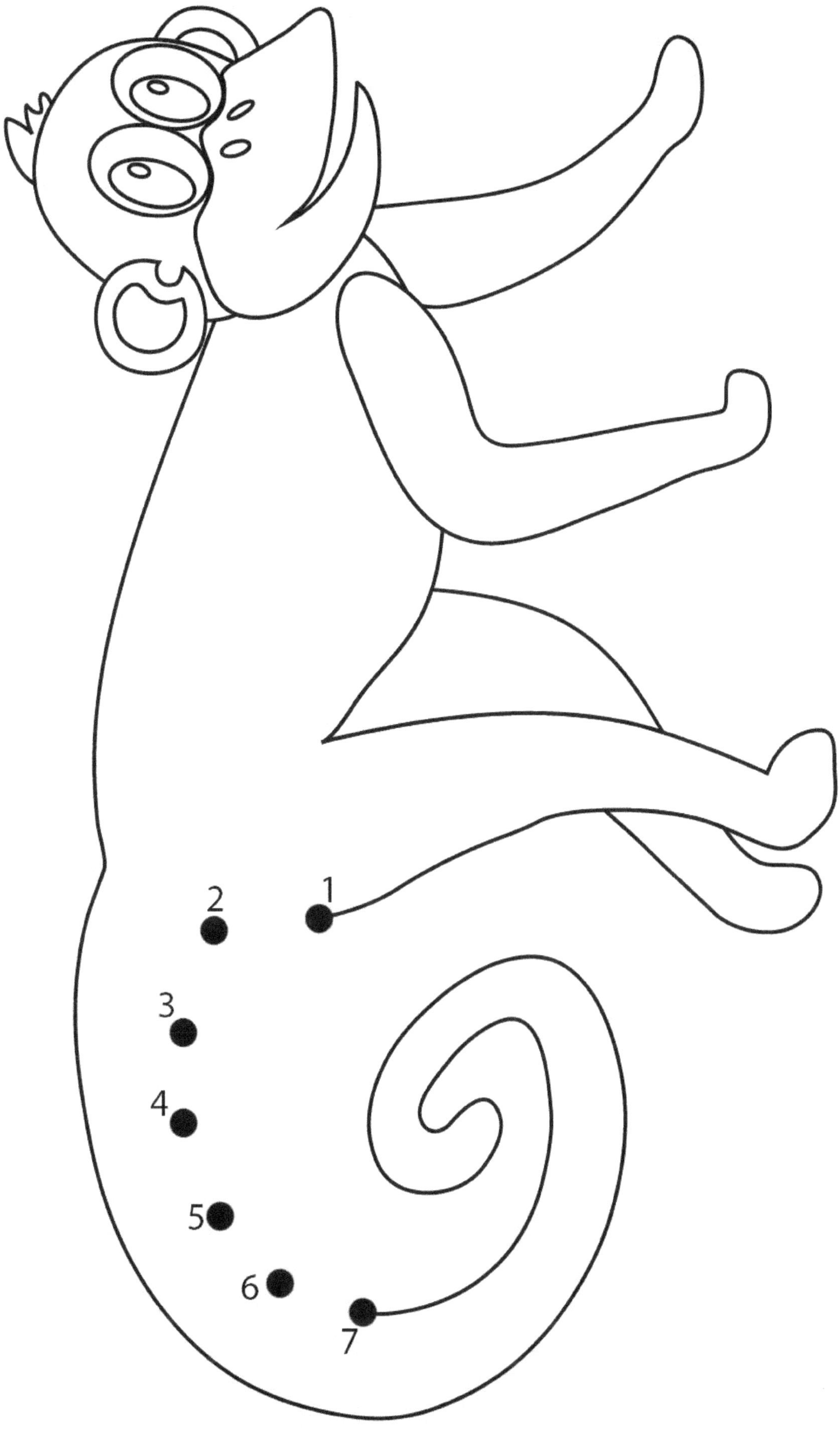
1
2
3
4
5
6
7

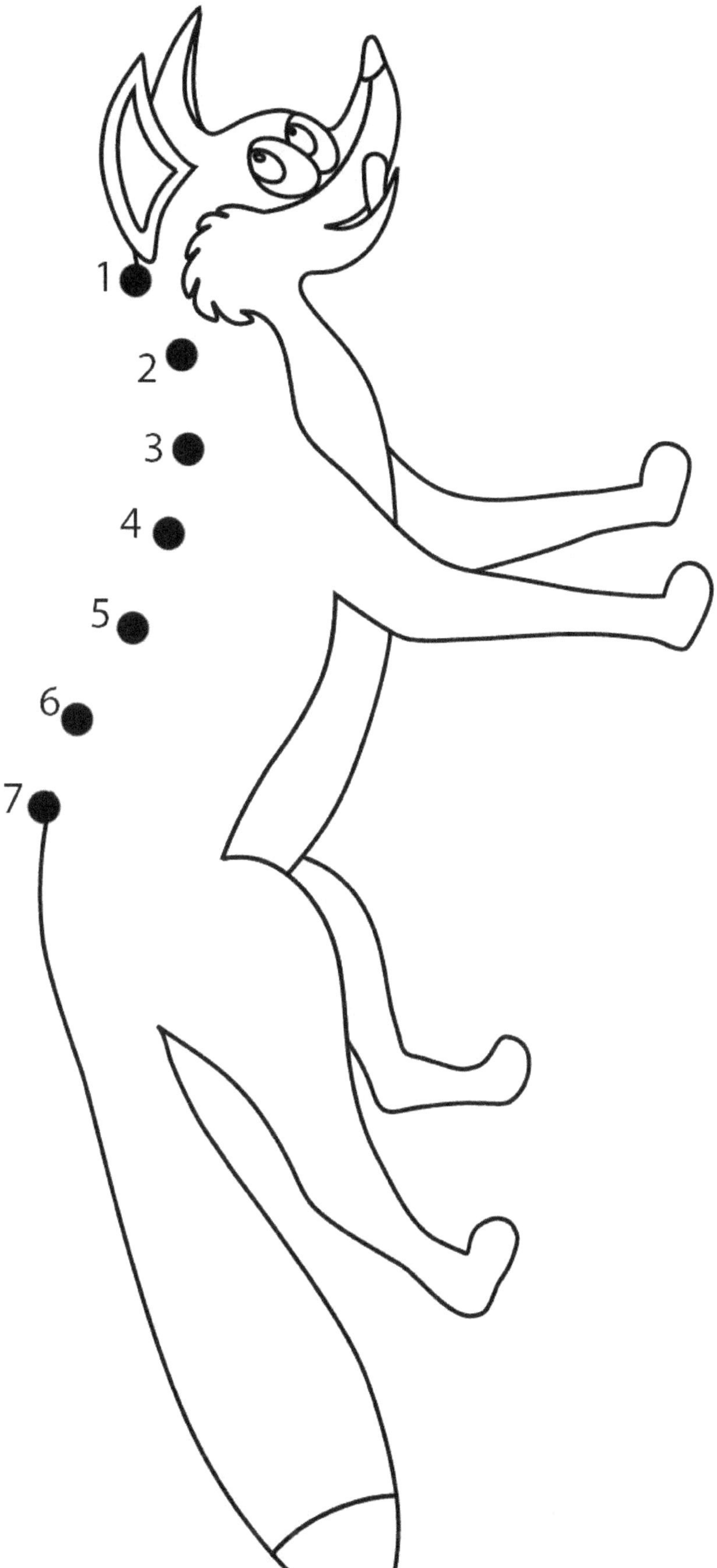
1
2
3
4
5
6
7

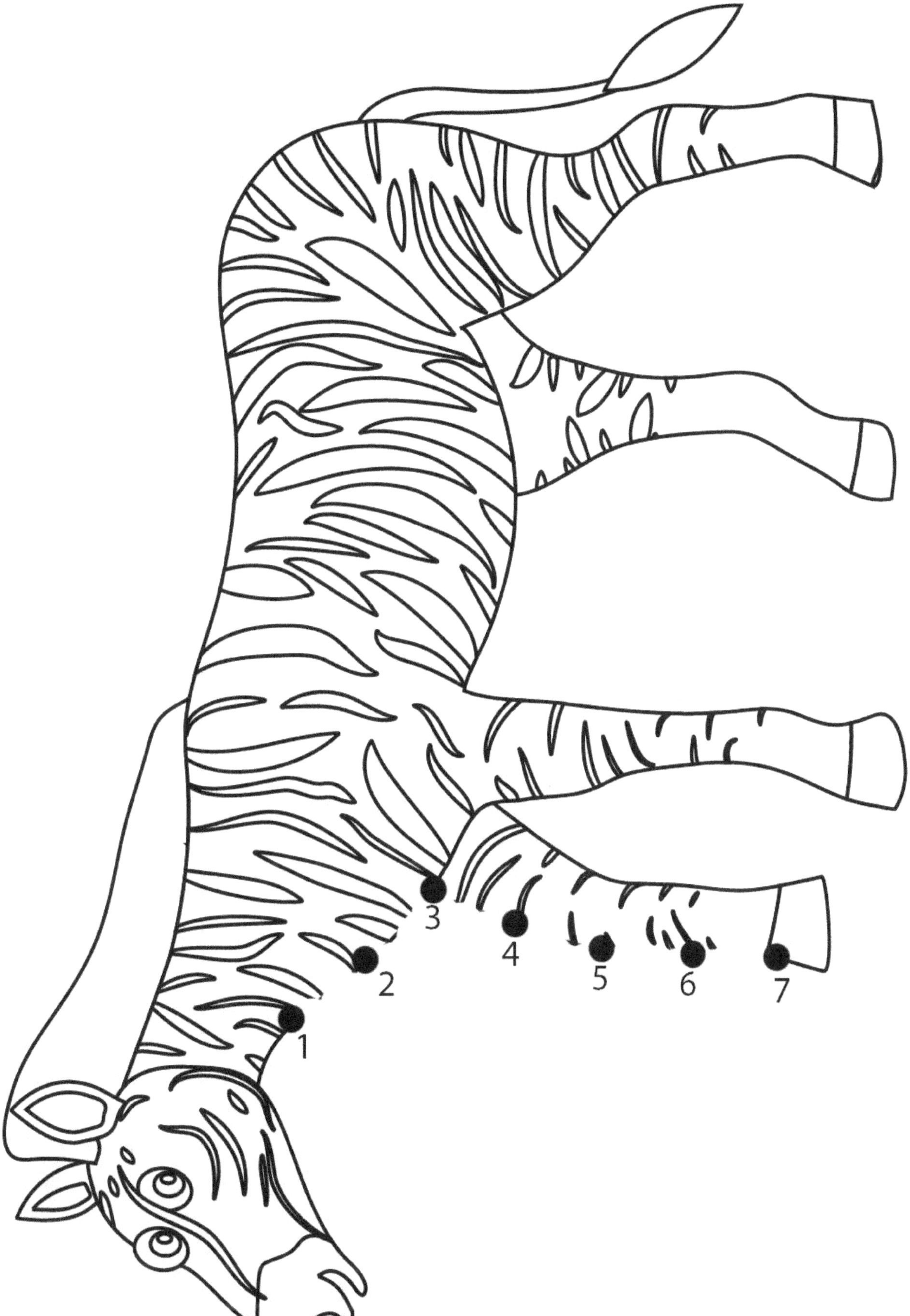
1
2
3
4
5
6
7

1
2
3
4
5
6
7

1
2
3
4
5
6
7

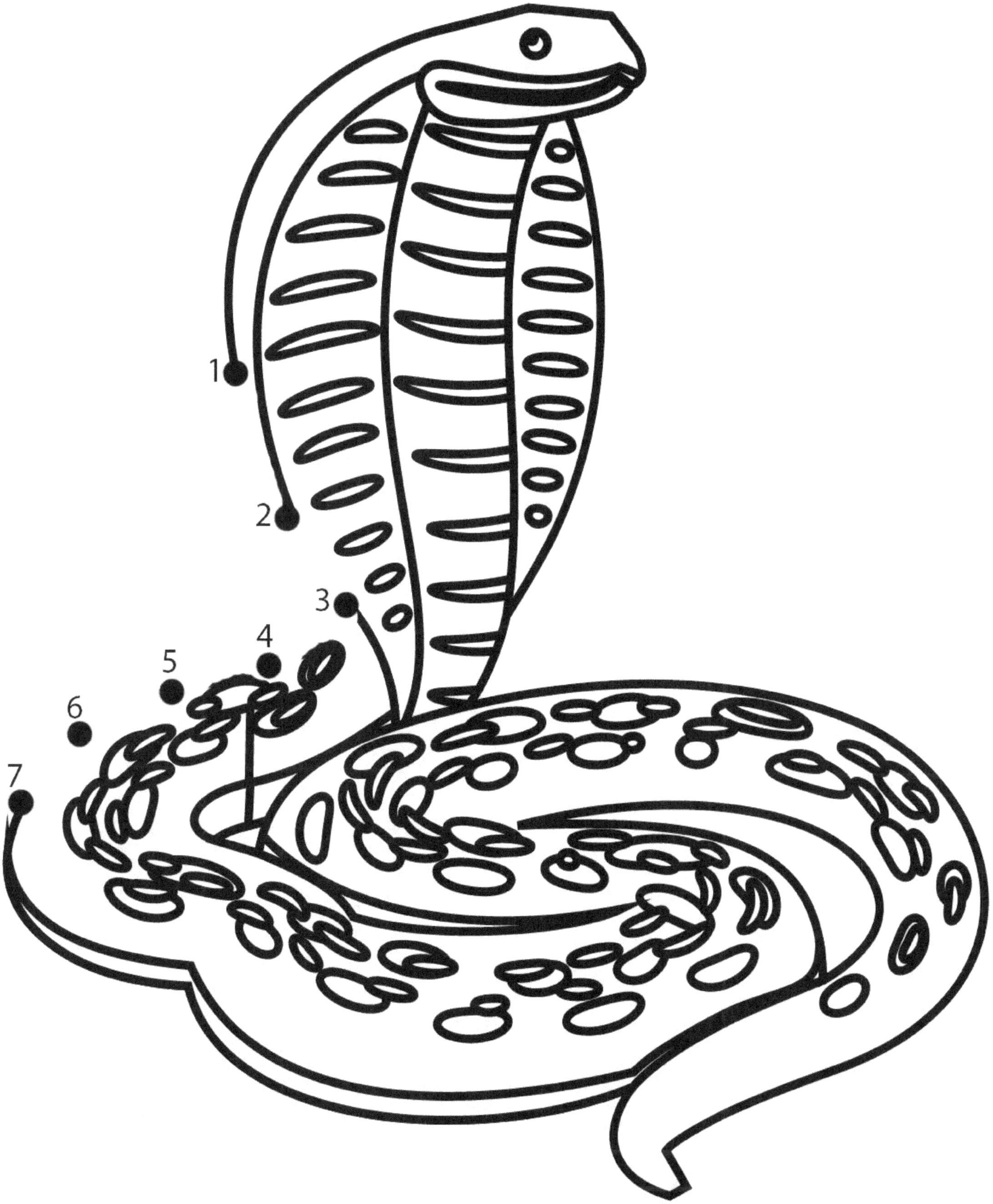
1
2
3
4
5
6
7

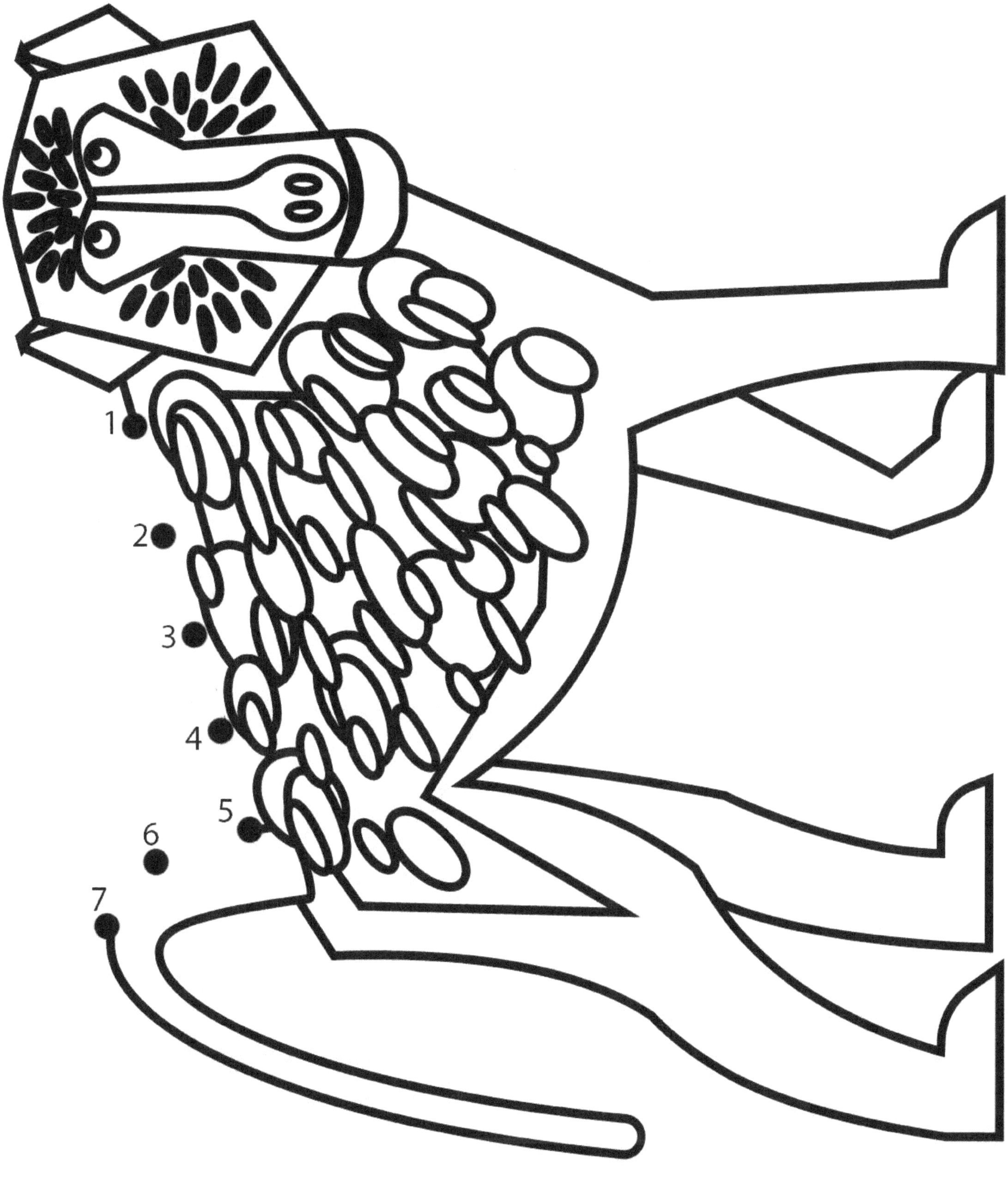
1
2
3
4
5
6
7

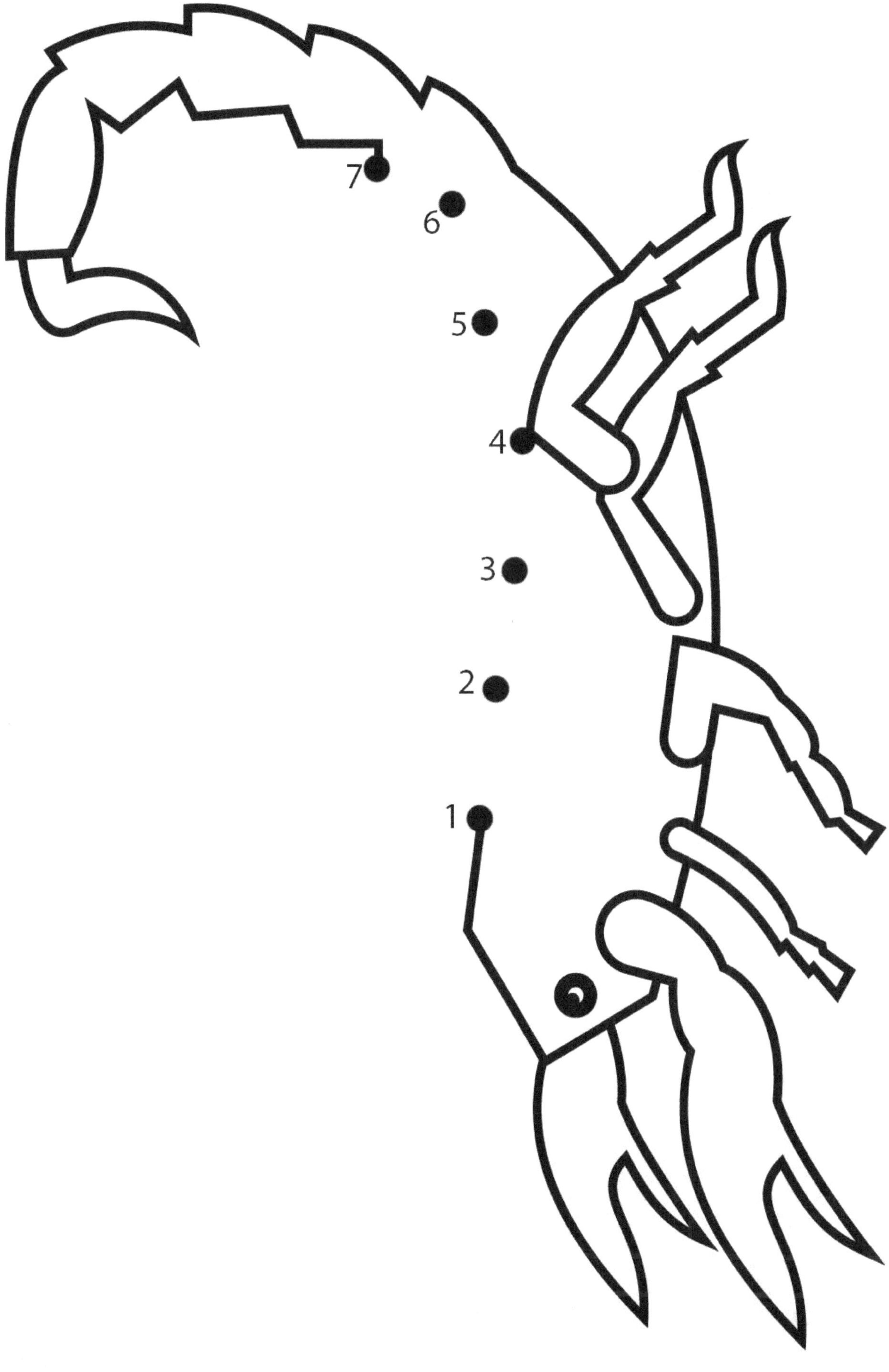
7
6
5
4
3
2
1

1
2
3
4
5
6
7

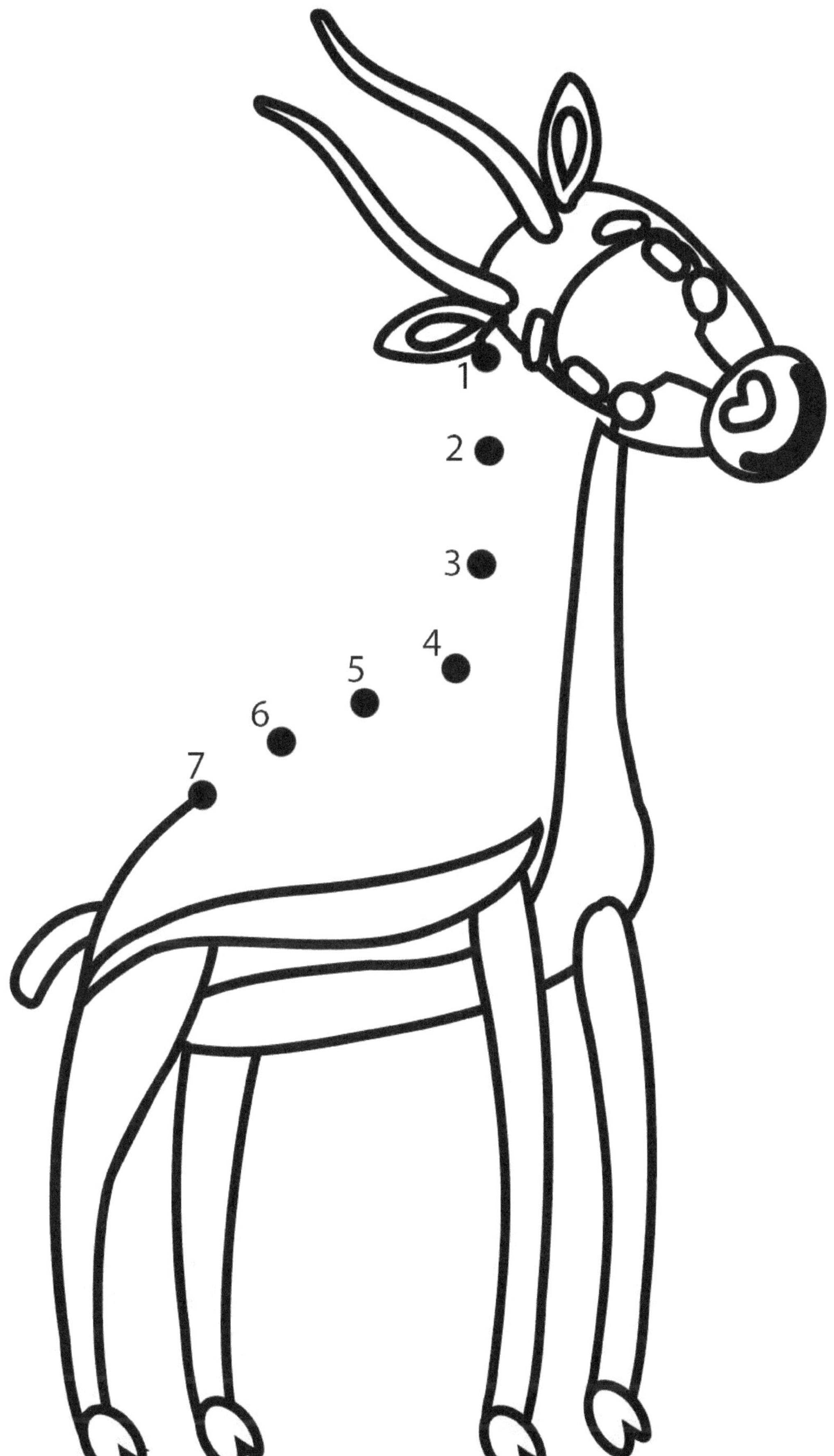
1
2
3
4
5
6
7

1
2
3
4
5
6
7

1
2
3
4
5
6
7

www.ingramcontent.com/pod-product-compliance
Lightning Source LLC
Chambersburg PA
CBHW081541220526
45467CB00010B/3284
9798728137566

Hope you enjoy this
Dot-to-Dot Coloring Book.

Thank you.